STANDING ON OUR LAST BONES

Written by
NGONIDZASHE DIANA JOHNS

Conscious Dreams
PUBLISHING

Standing on Our Last Bones

Copyright © 2025: Ngonidzashe Diana Johns

All rights reserved. No part of this publication may be produced, distributed, or transmitted in any form or by any means, including photocopying, recording, or other electronic or mechanical methods, without the prior written permission of the publisher, except in the case of brief quotations embodied in critical reviews and certain other non-commercial uses permitted by copyright law.

Published by Conscious Dreams Publishing
www.consciousdreamspublishing.com

Edited by Daniella Blechner and Elise Abram
Typeset and E-book formatting by Amit Dey
Cover Design by Emily's World of Design

ISBN: 978-1-917584-66-1

DEDICATION

To my Gogo, forever in my bones, whose love still lights the path.

To my sisters and my mother, for holding me, loving me without condition & carrying me when I could not stand.

To my golden girls, you know yourselves, lifting me up in prayer, in faith, in unwavering love.

To my beloved new sisters, in this chronic illness journey, for walking with me through unseen battles and holding space for our scars.

To the unheard, the misdiagnosed, the neglected, whose voices are silenced but whose spirits refuse to bow.

To those fighting injustice in the health system and beyond, who rise when the world refuses to see.

To God, the real One, my body may break, bruise, and falter, but my spirit will not.

To the ones who choose to stand when all else fails, to witness, to resist, to rise—this is for you.

May these pages honour our courage, our fury, our love, and the sacred power of STANDING on OUR LAST BONES and still rising.

TABLE OF CONTENTS

Dedication. iii
Prologue: A Tapestry of Twenty-Eight. ix

CHAPTER 1: My Gogo - Jessina Norah Nyabunze 1

   Grief, Loss & Chronic Illness 1
   Laughter's Echo 3
   Remembrance Hymn. 4
   Gogo's Lullaby 5
   Whispers of the Shadowed Souls 6
   Echoes of Loss. 7
   Barren Bloom 10
   Vilomah 12
   A Mother's Star. 14
   Phoenix Rising 16

CHAPTER 2: Family, Kinship & Reconnection 17

   Sisterhood's Tapestry. 18
   An Aunt's Heart 19

The Joy of Kinship. 20

Faded Tapestry 21

Lost in Shadows 22

A Call for Reconnection 23

CHAPTER 3: Identity, Empowerment & Heritage 25

Legacy of Rage. 27

Beyond the Stereotype 28

Independent Woman. 29

Golden Hour Women 31

Golden Age Goddesses 32

CHAPTER 4: Resilience And Strength. 33

Phoenix Rising 35

Resilience Rising 36

Daughter of Strength 38

Breaking Free 39

Forged in Fire 41

Symphonies of Triumph 43

CHAPTER 5: Love & Relationships 45

Love's Paradox 47

Unmatched Rhythms. 49

Shattered Reflections. 50

Captive Heart. 51

Ferrero Rocher Love 52

Betrayal's Bite. 53

Rambling Plea 54

Shifting Tides. 55

CHAPTER 6: Nature & Introspection 57

Steady Pulse of Life 57

Forged in Nature 59

Zora's Eden. 60

Night's Prisoner 61

England's Soul 62

A Solitary Bloom. 63

A Beacon in the Storm. 64

Fractured Reflections. 65

CHAPTER 7: Breath Unbound, Knees and
Echoes of Loud Silence Rising 67

Breathless and Bound 69

Breath Held, Fists Raised 71

Mama Answers Back 74

Resilience Rising 77

Shattered Reflections 78

Shackled Spirit, Soaring Soul. 79

Ignite 80

Zora's Storm 81

CHAPTER 8: Embers of Becoming, Ashes & Alters 83

    A Fourteen-Year-Old's Awakening. 85

    Twenty-Five 86

    Roora Ritual 87

    Wheel It to Will It 88

    Divine Refuge 89

    Our Journey's Page. 90

    Evolution of Expression. 92

    The Writer's Odyssey. 93

    Standing on Our Last Bones. 94

About the Author. 97

> **PROLOGUE**

A TAPESTRY OF TWENTY-EIGHT

2022 was a year of unmasking. The gilded cage of adulthood, once believed impenetrable, crumbled under the weight of its own absurdity. With age came a curious paradox: a thirst for knowledge and a deepening introspection. Superficial concerns, like the tyranny of the scale, faded into insignificance as life's deeper questions emerged.

My relationship with the divine evolved into an intimate conversation, a friendship of sorts. At 28, the tunnel of existence stretched before me, its end obscured by shadows. The heart, a captive in this labyrinth, yearned for liberation. In those moments of profound vulnerability, a choice materialised: succumb or transcend.

I chose life.

With deliberate intent, I cultivated peace, a sanctuary within the storm. Mental health became a sacred trust, nurtured with care. Prayer, once a ritual, transformed into a dialogue, a source of strength. Ambition ignited, not as a relentless pursuit, but as a purposeful journey. I learned to find joy in the unexpected, extracting lessons from life's intricate tapestry.

Hair fell, not as a victim, but as a canvas for a new identity. Control, an illusion, was relinquished with surprising ease. In its place bloomed a love for authentic connection, a hunger for intellectual stimulation.

This journey, marked by challenges, has forged a resilience I never knew existed. It's a story still unfolding, a narrative rich with contrast and growth. A story I share not for pity but for empathy and inspiration. This is not a tale of woe but a testament to the human spirit's resilience. When life's storms rage, finding an anchor amidst the chaos becomes paramount. This story is about discovering that anchor within oneself, about finding peace in the eye of the tempest. It's about pushing beyond perceived limitations and emerging stronger on the other side.

With my sisters and friends, I've made a pact: to live fully, to create memories that will echo through the years. As the laughter shared between ageing grandmothers, our stories, woven together, will be the fabric of our legacy.

When life hurls unexpected challenges, the true measure of an individual is revealed. Pushed to the brink, I discovered an inner strength I never knew existed. The rigid structures of multitasking gave way to a more fluid approach, demanding adaptability and resilience.

A deep-seated need for security led me to meticulously plan for life's uncertainties. Health insurance, income protection and life coverage became more than just policies; they were lifelines. While preparation didn't cushion the impact of adversity, it provided a sense of peace amidst the chaos.

This journey was a stark reminder that life is unpredictable. Yet, within its unpredictability lies an opportunity for extraordinary growth. It's a testament to the human spirit's capacity to endure, adapt, and ultimately triumph.

And so I write, not just to share but to understand, to process, to heal. To find solace in the shared human experience. To celebrate the resilience of the human spirit.

Theodore Roosevelt's exhortation to 'strive valiantly and dare greatly' has been a guiding star throughout the creation of this work. It is a spirit that permeates these pages, an invitation to embrace the extraordinary within the ordinary. The pages that follow are an invitation to enter the arena, to witness the triumphs and failures, the dust, sweat, and blood of a life lived fully. This is a story of striving valiantly, of daring greatly, and of finding strength in the face of adversity.

> "It is not the critic who counts: not the man who points out how the strong man stumbles or where the doer of deeds could have done better. The credit belongs to the man who is actually in the arena, whose face is marred by dust and sweat and blood, who strives valiantly, who errs and comes up short again and again, because there is no effort without error or shortcoming, but who knows the great enthusiasms, the great devotions, who spends himself in a worthy cause; who, at the best, knows, in the end, the triumph of high achievement, and who, at the worst, if he fails, at least he fails while daring greatly, so that his place shall never be with those cold and timid souls who knew neither victory nor defeat."
>
> —Theodore Roosevelt

CHAPTER 1

MY GOGO - JESSINA NORAH NYABUNZE

GRIEF, LOSS & CHRONIC ILLNESS

In Shona, we call our grandmother **Gogo** — the root from which so many branches rise. She called me **Bhodhi** — "bra," because I held her up, brought out her best features, and made her feel seen and beautiful. That was our secret language of devotion.

"If love alone could conquer death, our departed would still walk among us."

This poignant assertion from Grey's Anatomy reverberates within me. It's a truth as stark as it is sorrowful. The idea that love in its purest, most unconditional form is insufficient to defy mortality is a bitter pill to swallow. On 17 July 2021, she laid her body down to rest, and the world tilted. I had been prepared, but never ready.

This section holds that absence, its ache and its grace. It is an altar for all who have loved fiercely and still lost, for those navigating illness, for those who know the body can be broken but the spirit refuses to bow.

Enter these pages gently. They are elegy and witness, lament and survival. They remember Jessina Norah Nyabunze as she truly was fierce, tender, radiant — and they carry her legacy forward. May grief carry you, not drown you. May the love of our lost grandmother return as courage. May illness teach your spirit to shine — a quiet pulse of presence still holding us as we STAND ON OUR LAST BONES.

LAUGHTER'S ECHO

Oh, to have captured moments pure and bright,
Your laughter's melody, a sunlit light.
A treasure trove of memories I yearn,
In the heart, where love's embers burn.

Life's canvas painted with strokes unseen,
A masterpiece of moments, serene and keen.
With every year, your spirit grows near,
In whispered echoes, love conquers fear.

A legacy of love, a guiding star,
Inspiring dreams from near and far.
Though images may fade, your love endures,
A timeless tapestry, forever pure.

So, let the world know this heartfelt plea,
Of Grandma's love, wild and free.
Her spirit lives, a radiant flame,
In hearts connected, forever the same.

REMEMBRANCE HYMN

I craved to capture moments pure and bright,
Your laughter's echo, a guiding light.
But memories, like stardust, softly gleam,
A treasured trove, a cherished dream.

With each anniversary, a bittersweet art,
Your spirit lingers close to my heart.
A hymn, a melody, a soulful sound,
In every note, your love is found.

You taught me harmony, a sacred art,
A symphony of faith, a soulful start.
Your voice, a beacon through life's darkest night,
Guiding my steps with love's pure light.

Now, hymns are echoes of a time gone by,
Tears and laughter, where memories lie.
A bittersweet longing, a soulful pain,
To hear your voice, to feel you near again.

I see your smile in every sacred verse,
A love so boundless, a universe immersed.
Your legacy lives on in every breath,
A testament to love, conquering death.

In quiet moments, your spirit I embrace,
A gentle whisper in life's endless chase.
Through hymns, I'll cherish your memory's art,
Forever etched deep in my heart.

GOGO'S LULLABY

In realms of sorrow, where hearts yearn and mend,
A bond forged in love, a timeless friend.
A grandchild's spirit, with Grandma entwined,
A tapestry of memories deeply enshrined.

Unconditional love, a river's steady flow,
Through seasons of life, their spirits grow.
A legacy cherished, a guiding star,
Inspiring dreams from near and far.

Through corridors of time, her spirit roams,
Carrying echoes of Grandma's gentle tones.
A beacon of faith, a steadfast light,
Dispelling shadows with morning's bright.

With every dawn, a promise to fulfil,
Grandma's love, a powerful will.
A garden of kindness where hearts take root,
Nourished by memories, a hopeful fruit.

When shadows creep, and doubts arise,
Grandma's wisdom, a sweet surprise.
A love transcending time and space,
A tender smile, a warm embrace.

On anniversaries, tears may fall,
 But Grandma's spirit answers the call.
A symphony of love, a soulful art,
Forever etched, deep in the heart.

WHISPERS OF THE SHADOWED SOULS

Death's bitter scent, a haunting, acrid stain,
Echoes of '20, '21, relentless pain.
Grief's tempest rages, a soul adrift at sea,
Yet, in the darkness, hope begins to be.

To dwell in sorrow, a shadowed, empty space,
 Is to deny the living, life's swift pace.
True honour lies not in mournful, endless night,
But in the dawning of a hopeful light.

A fragile thread, life's delicate art,
Revealed in loss, a broken, wounded heart.
Tears fall like rain, a ceaseless, mournful sound,
Yet, in the depths, resilience can be found.

The hurried grave, a stark and final scene,
A poignant reminder of what once has been.
But in remembrance, let compassion reside,
Honour the spirit, where souls abide.

Hope, like a beacon, in shadows deep,
Ignites the soul from sorrow's slumbering sleep.
To live and love with purpose, heart, and mind,
A legacy to leave for all mankind.

With kindred spirits, we find solace, grace,
To mend the heart, to find a healing place.
Through darkest hours, let courage be our guide,
Emerging stronger on life's hopeful tide.

ECHOES OF LOSS

The acrid scent of loss clung to the air,
a haunting relic of 2020 and 2021.
Pain, a relentless tyrant, threatened to consume,
but we must resist its dominion.

To erect monuments to suffering is to be imprisoned by it.
It is a common fallacy to believe that clinging to sorrow honours the departed.
True reverence resides in living fully,
even amidst the tempest of grief.

Loss awakens us to life's fragility,
urging us to cherish each moment with those we love.
Grief is a tempestuous sea,
with waves of laughter and tears.

It demands community, empathy and time.
We must permit ourselves
to feel the full spectrum of emotion,
ultimately finding solace and joy anew.

The hurried descent of loved ones into the earth
is a stark, brutal truth.
We must implore for tenderness,
for recognition of the soul within the casket.

The haste, the absence of ritual,
is a poignant reminder of life's impermanence.
Yet hope endures.
The belief in reunion fuels our spirits.

We grieve,
but we do not surrender.
We live, we love, we strive;
This is our truest tribute.

In the shadows of despair,
our tribe becomes our sanctuary.
Through toil and aspiration,
We heal and renew.

We are defined not by sorrow,
But by resilience, hope, and the unwavering belief in a brighter dawn.
In the depths of grief,
We discover our strength.
Numbed and Rebirthed
Midnight's hush, a solitary chime,
One letter at a time, defying time.
Cubital's grip, a numbing, cruel art,
As healing words mend my wounded heart.

A fragile hand, once nimble and free,
Now bound by pain, a captive decree.
Each finger, a missing piece of me,
In silent longing, a soul's plea.

Grateful now for senses oft-ignored,
The warmth of skin, a treasure hoard
With every letter, a small victory,
As mind and body find their harmony.

In darkest hours, a flicker of light,
Rebirth of movement, a hopeful sight.
With every keystroke, a spirit's mend,
A new chapter where strength transcends.

BARREN BLOOM

In the silence of my barren womb,
A desert blooms, a thorny tomb.
Echoes of laughter, once a dream,
Replaced by shadows, a mournful theme.

The blood that flows, a crimson tide,
Washes hopes away, where dreams abide.
Sanitary pads a stark reminder,
Of a future lost, a hope enshrined.

God's irony, a cruel jest,
A barren womb, a life suppressed.
I yearn for children, a mother's role,
But pain and silence claim my soul.

A cactus heart, where dreams reside,
In shadows deep, I'll try to hide.
Yet hope remains, a flicker's gleam,
In this desolate, maternal dream.

Endometriosis's Shadow

Endometriosis, a silent foe,
A battle waged where shadows grow.
The pain it brings, a constant ache,
A heavy burden, hard to break.

Sanitary pads, a costly shield,
Against a pain that will not yield.
Dreams of motherhood, a distant star,
Torn apart by life's unfair war.

A Christian's faith, a hopeful plea,
But pain's reality sets spirits free.
To find solace, the strength to endure,
In hope's embrace, a future secure.

With every month, a fresh despair,
A silent battle, a constant care.
But in the darkness, a light may shine,
A flicker of hope, a life divine.

VILOMAH

In sorrow's chasm, where shadows intertwine,
A mother's heart, a fractured, mournful shrine,
Vilomah echoes, a haunting, mournful plea,
A child's lost laughter, a haunting memory.

Like petals scattered by a tempest's ire,
A life extinguished, a soul's funeral pyre,
Tears, like rivers, carve canyons of despair,
As echoes of joy turn to mournful air.

A stone-like weight upon her weary breast,
A silent world where shadows are her guests,
Yearning for solace, a touch, a whispered name,
A love eternal, consuming her like a flame.

Yet in the darkness, hope's ember glows,
A flicker of light where memory softly flows,
A refuge found in dreams where spirits meet,
A bond unbroken, eternally sweet.

Though grief's tempest rages, her love endures,
A steadfast beacon through sorrow's darkest lures,
For in her heart, the child forever lives,
A testament to love, that hope is alive.

So let us gather with gentle, tender care,
To share her burden, her sorrow to bear,
With empathy's embrace, let healing start,
To mend her broken heart and soothe her shattered part.

A MOTHER'S STAR

In sorrow's ocean, depths profound and vast,
A mother's heart, a shattered, fragile cast,
A love once radiant, now a mournful gleam,
A child's departure, a heart-wrenching dream.

With lullabies woven of starlight and air,
She cradled her treasure beyond compare,
A beacon of hope in life's darkest hour,
A bond unbreakable, love's enduring power.

But fate, a cruel sculptor, chiselled her pain,
A silent world where echoes softly strain,
An empty cradle, a haunting, vacant space,
Tears like rivers, eroding time's embrace.

In memories' gardens, she seeks solace deep,
Where laughter echoes, gentle vigils keep,
Yet shadows lengthen as twilight descends,
A heart adrift where sorrow never ends.

In dreams, they reunite on celestial shore,
Where time stands still, forevermore,
A love transcendent, a bond pure and bright,
Guiding her spirit through the darkest night.

With dawn's embrace, she rises, bravely strong,
Though grief's tempestuous waves desire.
Her child's spirit, a star in her soul's sky,
Ignites hope's ember, burning ever high.

So, let us gather with hearts pure and deep,
To cradle her spirit from sorrow to keep,
With empathy's balm, let healing commence,
To mend her heart in gentle recompense.

PHOENIX RISING

Once a bustling kingdom, now a silent shore,
Comrades departed, echoes evermore.
A queen dethroned, stripped of her golden hair,
Yet from the ashes, a phoenix takes the air.

No mourning for lost adornments, no borrowed grace;
Tempered by trials, I've carved my own place.
A crown of scars, forged in blood and sweat,
A queen reborn, a debt to self I'll not forget.

The depths of sorrow, a tempestuous sea;
Yet in the silence, strength grows in me.
A flicker of hope, a beacon in the night,
Transforming darkness into guiding light.

When shadows lengthen and doubt draws near,
I summon the warrior within, stilling each fear.
Let rain fall and nourish the soul's hidden seed—
A garden of courage, blooming from need.

With courage as armour and hope as my shield,
I rise from the tempest and claim life's field.
For in the darkness, stars begin to gleam—
A phoenix ascendant, fulfilling life's dream.

❯ CHAPTER 2

FAMILY, KINSHIP & RECONNECTION

Before we ever had words, we had touch, lullabies, the soft braid of hands and histories. Here live the ones who raised us, the ones we raised, the ones we've lost and still carry.

This section is a map of that terrain — parent and child calling across silence, aunt and niece threading joy between miles, sisters weaving light through distance, grandmothers planting a fierce legacy in soil that never forgets our names.

These poems are not portraits in glass. They breathe. They ache. They mend. They remember and they reach. Step into them as you would a homecoming: with open palms, with the courage to look at what has frayed, with the hope that kinship, like water, finds its way back to the root.

And as you walk these pages, may you feel the marrow of belonging rising beneath you. May every break find its mend. Every memory turns to kindness and lineage becomes light on your path — steadying you as we STAND ON OUR LAST BONES.

SISTERHOOD'S TAPESTRY

Bound by blood, a tapestry we weave,
Hearts entwined where souls believe.
Miles may part, but spirits soar,
A sister's love, forevermore.

From childhood dreams to adult strife,
Our bond endures, a precious life.
Through laughter, tears and shared delight,
Our sisterhood shines, a guiding light.

Across the years, our hearts still yearn,
For moments shared where spirits burn.
With every call, a bridge we mend,
Our love's foundation, without end.

From grandmothers' grace, a legacy sown,
A love so fierce, a steadfast throne.
We'll pass this bond through generations bright,
A sister's heart, a guiding light.

So let us cherish this sacred tie,
With love's embrace, let spirits fly.
A sisterhood unyielding, strong and true,
Our hearts united, you and me.

AN AUNT'S HEART

A tapestry of love where hearts entwine,
With nieces and nephews, a joy divine.
Their laughter like music, a sweet refrain,
Filling my days with sunshine's warm rain.

In their young eyes, the world's wonder gleams,
Inspiring dreams like hopeful beams.
A guiding star, a steady hand to hold,
As their stories unfold, a tale untold.

With every giggle, my heart takes flight,
In their presence, everything feels right.
A bond unbreakable, a love so deep,
As guardian angel, their spirits I'll keep.

Though miles may part us, our hearts remain near,
 A love so profound, dispelling fear.
In their growth and triumphs, I'll always share,
A steadfast anchor beyond compare.

THE JOY OF KINSHIP

A circle of love where hearts entwine,
With aunts and nieces, a bond divine.
Their laughter a melody, sweet and clear,
Filling life's canvas with joy sincere.

In their young eyes, a world of dreams takes flight,
Inspiring futures with all their might.
A guiding star, a constant friend,
On life's journey, their spirits to mend.

With every moment, a treasure to hold,
In stories shared, where memories unfold.
A love so boundless, a heart's embrace,
In this kinship, I find my place.

Though distance may challenge, our bond endures,
A steadfast connection, forever pure.
In their growth and triumphs, I'll always cheer,
A loving presence, dispelling fear.

FADED TAPESTRY

In childhood's garden, where our souls entwined,
A parent's love, a masterpiece designed,
Your laughter, sunlight on a summer's day,
Now shrouded in mist, a fading, distant grey.

Once a bright beacon guiding through the night,
Your spirit now veiled, a shadowed, cryptic sight.
Life's tempestuous seas have weathered your soul,
Dimming the fire, leaving embers to console.

Yet deep within this heart, a flame still gleams,
A love unwavering through life's shifting scenes.
Though oceans part us and mountains intervene,
My spirit reaches, yearning to convene.

Like shattered glass, our bond lies in despair,
Yearning for solace, for tenderest care.
With hope as a compass, we'll navigate the sea,
To mend our tapestry, wild and free.

LOST IN SHADOWS

In youth's tender embrace, a bond once formed,
A parent's love, a world where hearts are warmed,
In laughter's echo and joy's sweet song,
Together in love, we both did belong.

But time, like waves upon a rocky shore,
Has shaped us both, changed us forevermore,
A parent, once kind and full of delight,
Now shrouded in shadows, hidden from sight.

Your heart, once open, is now closed and cold,
The love that once flowed now seems to withhold,
But know, dear parent, in my heart, it's true,
No matter the distance, my love for you grew.

Through trials and woes that life has unfurled,
I hold onto memories, your love's bright pearl,
For though you've changed, the love I feel inside,
An ember that refuses to subside.

A CALL FOR RECONNECTION

Innocence lost and childhood's sweet embrace,
I long for those moments, that familiar place,
But I won't give up, for hope still resides,
That we can reconnect, heal what divides.

Let's bridge the chasm, mend what's been torn,
Rekindle the love that was once cherished.
For deep in my heart, the love remains strong,
A parent and child forever belong.

Though time has transformed us, we still can mend,
Our bond, our connection, our love's precious blend,
So, let's reach out with open hearts anew,
Rediscover the love that will see us through.

CHAPTER 3

IDENTITY, EMPOWERMENT & HERITAGE

> **Here is the fire after the grief, the voice after the whisper, the body standing whole after being named a wound.**
>
> This section is a gathering of our many selves — the Golden Hour women stepping into their own light, the independent ones carrying bills and burdens with grace, the goddesses of the golden age redefining power, the ones who burn through stereotype and silence, the descendants who hold rage as inheritance and alchemise it into freedom.
>
> These poems are not apologies. They are declarations, drumbeats of memory and becoming, rooted in Zimbabwean soil, braided with global sisterhood. They honour the women who have come before and call forth the ones yet to rise.
>
> Step into them ready to be witnessed and to witness. Step into them as a ceremony of reclamation. Each line is an ember of heritage, each stanza a doorway into your own strength.

And as the pages open, may you feel your spine lengthen, your name deepen, your ancestors stir — reminding you that identity is not a mask but a crown you inherit and remake.

May the names you carry become music, not weight. May every stereotype turned to ash reveal the bright metal of your truth. May the rage of your foremothers become a wind at your back, not a chain at your feet. May you walk into the world wearing your heritage like morning light — not hidden, but radiating.

And when you forget who you are, may these words bring you home to the strength, the grace, and the endless lineage of love that still holds you steady as we **STAND ON OUR LAST BONES.**

LEGACY OF RAGE

My anger, forged in whips and stolen grace,
A searing brand upon my people's faces.
Inhaling deeply, I taste ancestral pain,
A hunger for freedom driving me insane.

A bittersweet symphony, my soul's lament,
Echoes of bondage, deeply indent.
A slave's great-granddaughter, I bear the weight,
Of centuries of wrong, a bitter fate.

'A mistake,' your lips betray a callous art,
Ignorance echoes a stone-cold heart.
Four hundred years of silence, now a scream,
A rising tempest, a defiant dream.

BEYOND THE STEREOTYPE

Ignorance echoes, a jarring refrain,
A twisted image, a painful stain.
'Sweet face, fiery tongue,' a shallow decree,
A stereotypical grip stifling me?
'Smile more,' they demand, a patronising art,
Unmasking the anger, a wounded heart.
Dracarys whispers, a defiant flame,
Incinerating prejudice, a cleansing aim.

I am more than a mask, a complex soul,
A story untold, beyond their control.
So, let the stereotype crumble and fall,
A black woman rising, answering the call.

INDEPENDENT WOMAN

Borrowing Maya Angelou's voice, I declare,
My independence, a birthright, laid bare.

Bills and burdens, I shoulder with grace,
Like Tubman, I carry the world's heavy case.

Strong, brave, and humble, a complex blend,
3 a.m. prayers for strength to transcend.

Boss, wife, and maid, a juggling art,
A warrior's spirit, a tender heart.

Vision and courage, my guiding light,
Breaking chains of oppression and night.

Patience and wisdom, my steady hand,
Building communities across the land.

Michelle's boldness, Rosa's brave core,
Defying bullies forevermore.
Humble in spirit yet fiercely bold,
My independence, a story untold.

So, spare your judgment, your negative gaze,
See beyond the surface in countless ways.

A mother, a sister, a friend, a wife,
An independent woman, filled with life.

Sojourner's truth echoes in my soul,
A proud spirit, complete and whole.

Ngonidzashe Diana Johns

GOLDEN HOUR WOMEN

In twilight's hush, where shadows softly creep,
Women emerge, their spirits rise from sleep,
Beyond the blush of youth's exuberant bloom,
They find their strength, their radiance, their room.

Like rivers carving paths through ancient stone,
They've faced life's storms, not walked alone.
With hearts of gold and wisdom's guiding light,
They navigate the shadows into the day's bright light.

No longer bound by youth's capricious sway,
They've found their voice, their independent way.
Entrepreneurs, dreamers with purpose clear,
Defying norms, dispelling doubt and fear.

With every year, their beauty deepens, grows,
A tapestry of grace where love flows.
They stand as pillars, strong and astute,
Inspiring others with courage resolute.

So, let us honour these women, wise and bold,
Whose stories, like legends, are yet untold,
Illuminate our world with hope's warm gleam,
 A testament to strength, a woman's dream.

GOLDEN AGE GODDESSES

Beyond the blush of youth's fleeting grace,
A new dawn rises, illuminating space.
Fifty, sixty years of wisdom's art,
Ignite a passion, a thriving heart.

No longer bound by societal chains,
These women flourish in life's vibrant plains.
With courage as their shield, ambition's fire,
They soar to heights, reaching ever higher.

Entrepreneurs, leaders with spirits bold,
Their stories written in chapters untold.
Each wrinkle, a testament to the strength they've found,
In life's crucible, where souls are profound.

No longer defined by youth's fleeting charm,
They've mastered life's complex, intricate form.
With grace and power, they redefine their art,
Leaving footprints on history's heart.

Let us celebrate these women, strong and true,
Whose spirits shine a brilliant, radiant hue.
For in their prime, a golden age is found,
Where wisdom reigns, and joy resounds.

> CHAPTER 4

RESILIENCE AND STRENGTH

Before we ever called it courage, we called it breathing through storms, rising from ashes, refusing to be broken. Here live the ones who faced the tempest, the ones who loved fiercely despite fear, the ones who discovered their own strength in the quiet aftermath of loss. This section is a map of that terrain—heart to heart, spirit to spirit, the moments when love and hope refuse to leave, even as everything else falls away.

A queen dethroned, stripped of her golden hair, yet from the ashes a phoenix rises. A silent figure to the world unknown, yet within this heart, a strength is sown. A daughter of strength moves with purpose, carrying scars, love, and heritage alike.

May the courage you carry find its echo in every heartbeat. May the storms you have weathered water the roots of your spirit and may every shadow you meet teach you the depth of your light.

May your scars speak softly of survival, your tears nourish the gardens of hope, and your quiet triumphs rise like stars above the night. May the weight you bear be met with grace, the battles you fight be honoured, and the strength within you unfurl with gentle insistence.

May love, in all its forms, sustain you, and may your spirit, though tested, remain unshaken—undaunted, unbroken, unbound.

And as you turn these pages, may every fear soften, every scar hum with meaning, every quiet triumph echo in your chest—steadying you as we **STAND ON OUR LAST BONES.**

PHOENIX RISING

Once a bustling kingdom, now a silent shore,
Comrades departed, echoes evermore.
A queen dethroned, stripped of her golden hair,
Yet from the ashes, a phoenix takes the air.

No mourning for lost adornments, no borrowed grace;
Tempered by trials, I've carved my own place.
A crown of scars, forged in blood and sweat,
A queen reborn, a debt to self I'll not forget.

The depths of sorrow, a tempestuous sea;
Yet in the silence, strength grows in me.
A flicker of hope, a beacon in the night,
Transforming darkness into guiding light.

When shadows lengthen and doubt draws near,
I summon the warrior within, stilling each fear.
Let rain fall and nourish the soul's hidden seed—
A garden of courage, blooming from need.

With courage as armour and hope as my shield,
I rise from the tempest and claim life's field.
For in the darkness, stars begin to gleam—
A phoenix ascendant, fulfilling life's dream.

RESILIENCE RISING

Future self, heed this call,
I stand unwavering, facing it all.
God's grace surrounds, a steadfast keep,
Through darkest hours, I'll find my sleep.

A silent figure to the world unknown,
Yet within this heart, a strength is sown.
Battered and broken but spirit unchained,
Love's ember burning, steadfastly sustained.

Once a guiding star now lost in night,
My lover struggles with all his might.
Haunted echoes, a mournful chime,
His love in fragments through space and time.

I yearn for days when passion's fire burned bright,
When his love lifted me to soaring heights.
Now fear's cold hand upon his spirit lies,
As life's tempestuous waves endlessly rise.

In laughter's echoes, his essence I see,
A love concealed yet cherished by me.
With children's laughter, my heart finds grace,
Building a future at a steady pace.

To the world, I'll show a defiant face,
Unbroken spirit in life's swift race.
For in this love, a strength I'll find,
A love resilient of heart and mind.

DAUGHTER OF STRENGTH

I move with purpose, not whim or desire,
Solitude's balm when spirits retire.
Music's embrace, a healing retreat,
After life's battles, a sweet respite.

No hunger for want, a nourished soul,
Poverty's chapter, a story to control.
Betrayal's sting, a lesson well learned,
Resilience forged, where strength is earned.

A masterpiece crafted by nature's hand,
Confidence blooms in a promised land.
My father's daughter, a legacy borne,
In every step, a warrior reborn.

BREAKING FREE

Enveloped in shadows, a soul adrift and lone,
The world's scriptwriter, a silent, distant tone.
No role assigned, a mere spectator's part,
A wasted symphony, a broken heart.

Chained by doubt, a captive bird's despair,
A labyrinth of 'what ifs', a haunting snare.
Hope's ember fading, a flickering light,
Yet within the darkness, a resolute might.

From ashes of sorrow, a phoenix shall rise,
With newfound courage, a challenge to the skies.
To reclaim identity, a soul set free,
To paint life's canvas with bold artistry.

A tapestry woven with threads of gold,
No longer silenced, a story to be told.
With colours vibrant, resilience as the hue,
I'll forge my path; the world's old script I'll subdue.

No longer bound by expectations' chain,
I'll embrace the journey, conquer fear and pain.
With every step, a victory to claim,
My life, my narrative, a burning flame.

So, let them doubt, their words like empty air,
I'll rise above, with strength beyond compare.
A sovereign spirit, defiant and bold,
My destiny written, a story yet untold.

FORGED IN FIRE

In solitude's embrace, I find my voice,
A raw confession where shadows rejoice.
To share with the world, a vulnerable plea,
A quest for connection, authenticity.

Not for acclaim but for soul's release,
To find solace in words, a heart's sweet peace.
The critic's disdain, a fleeting affair,
The courageous heart, a standard to bear.

Nature's sculptor with wind and with rain,
Forges resilience through joy and through pain.
With every tempest, a spirit refined,
A masterpiece crafted, one of a kind.

She moulds, and she shapes with tenderest care,
A soul tempered by trials beyond compare.
In shadows of doubt, a flicker of hope,
A journey of growth where spirits elope.

With cunning and wisdom, she guides our way,
A cosmic architect, come what may.
Through fire and water, she tests our might,
Emerging triumphant in her guiding light.

With passion ignited and purpose defined,
A leader is born of resolute mind.
Through trials and triumphs, a legacy's made,
A testament to strength, where courage is laid.

When shadows engulf, and hope seems to flee,
A flicker of resilience sets the spirit free.
In the crucible of life, we're forged anew,
A masterpiece crafted, steadfast and true.

Nature's grand plan, a mystery untold,
A tapestry woven with threads of gold.
In her image, we strive to be,
A reflection of her divinity.

SYMPHONIES OF TRIUMPH

Awakened by sweat, the world a silent stage,
Regret's whisper echoes through the shadowed cage.
Shattered dreams and fading hopes, a bitter brew,
As we hurl accusations, old wounds renew.

A wasteland of potential, compromised and lost,
Like caged birds, our spirits pay a heavy cost.
The air, a suffocating weight of what could be,
A mournful symphony of despair's decree.

Yet from the ashes, a flicker, a spark ignites,
Resilience rising, challenging the darkest nights.
Within the wreckage, seeds of strength take root,
Yearning for sunlight, a hopeful pursuit.

Though silenced voices may echo in the mind,
Our spirits soar, defiant and defined.
In struggle's crucible, our power is found,
Transmuting anguish on wings unbound.

Scars like battle honours, worn with pride,
Reminders of courage, where hope resides.
For even in shadows, light can find its way,
Illuminating spirits, come what may.

Standing on our Last Bones

So, let us rise, fueled by inner fire's might,
Embrace the chaos, seize the dawning light.
No longer victims but architects of fate,
We'll rewrite our stories, seal destiny's gate.

United against despair's relentless tide,
We'll forge a path where hope and courage abide.
In adversity's dance, we'll find our grace,
Composing symphonies of triumph in life's space.

▷ CHAPTER 5

LOVE & RELATIONSHIPS

Before we had words, there was the brush of a hand, a heartbeat shared, a glance that lingered too long. Here live the loves that carried us, the ones that broke us open, the ones we held and the ones we had to let go. This section is a quiet room of memory and feeling—a place where joy and ache sit side by side, where longing meets tenderness, and where the pulse of love teaches us who we are.

A smile that lit the dark, a voice that soothed, a hand that stayed—or left. A flicker of warmth in frozen spaces. A phoenix rising quietly from heartbreak. These pages do not hold answers. They hold the hum of hearts, the courage to open again, the soft ache of loving fully, even when it leaves scars.

Step into these poems as you would a room filled with sunlight and shadow: with open palms, with patience for the tender ache, and with the quiet bravery to let love in, again and again.

May every love that has touched you leave a trace of grace. May every love that has gone teach you how to rise. May your heart, though tender, remember its own strength. May each whisper of connection, each fleeting joy, each remembered ache guide you gently, nourish you quietly, and awaken the courage to love again. May your spirit remain open—undaunted, unbroken, ready for love's endless possibilities.

And as you turn these pages, may every longing, every memory, every tender ache steady you as we **STAND ON OUR LAST BONES.**

LOVE'S PARADOX

A paradox of joy and ache,
Love's tapestry, a heart awake.
From knight in shining armour to a stark disguise,
I offered all, a lover's prize.

Your heart, a fortress, cold and deep,
While mine a vessel, yearning to weep.
I craved your warmth, your guiding light,
But found, instead, an endless night.

Shattered pieces, a love's despair,
Yet, in the wreckage, a flicker of care.
I sought a haven, a loving embrace,
Found icy depths, a desolate space.

A shattered mirror, love's reflection,
Lost in a maze, a soul's direction.
A tapestry woven with hope's bright thread,
Unravelled dreams where shadows tread.

I poured my soul, a selfless art,
Met with indifference, a broken heart.
Yet in the ruins, hope endures,
A phoenix rising, healing the sores.

Love's alchemy, a mystic art,
Transforming pain, a brand-new start.
Though scars remain, a testament's trace,
I find solace in love's embrace.

A journey shared through darkest hours,
Love's resilience, a blooming flower.
No answers sought for love's unknown,
On this journey, I'll walk alone.

A masterpiece etched with every scar,
Love's paradox forever afar.

UNMATCHED RHYTHMS

You were ready, a heart prepared to bind,
While mine wandered, lost and undefined.
A love ignited, a promise unspoken,
Yet timing's cruel hand, our paths broken.

She fits the mould, a wife in every way,
Whilst I remain a ghost of yesterday.
Two hearts entwined by fate's unfair decree,
A tragic sonnet, lost to memory.

SHATTERED REFLECTIONS

A silent echo in a world of noise,
A broken vessel where sorrow destroys.
With every cruel word, a piece of me dies,
A fragile spirit beneath shadowed skies.

Once a beacon, my lover's gleam dims,
Haunted by shadows, a fractured limb.
His love, a puzzle with missing parts,
A wounded soul torn by life's harsh darts.

I yearn for the days of passion's pure fire,
When his love lifted me higher and higher.
Now fear's icy fingers grip his heart,
As life's burdens tear our love apart.

Yet in his laughter, a glimpse of him shines,
A love hidden deep, where hope entwines.
I hold our memories, a cherished keep,
While praying for love's healing sleep.

So, to the world, I'll stand tall and proud,
A woman unbroken, though in shadows shroud.
I love a man, though storms may reside,
Our love's foundation, where hope will abide.

CAPTIVE HEART

A prisoner of memory, a captive heart,
Your ghost still lingers, playing its part.
Armoured defences, a fragile façade,
As remnants of love, a bittersweet load.

A maze of crumbs, a tantalising deceit,
A spicy allure, a bitter defeat.
Allergic to pain yet trapped in the past,
A prisoner's dilemma, forever amassed.

FERRERO ROCHER LOVE

Her smile, a golden, sweet cascade,
Electric chills, a thrilling masquerade.
Tongue's delight as flavours unfold,
A love story yet to be told.

A crowded market, a heart on display,
Hours of waiting, come what may.
Ferrero Rocher, a taste of desire,
Igniting passions, a soulful fire.

Syrupy sweetness, a velvet caress,
Rough edges softened, life's bittersweetness.
A love so rare, a precious find,
Beyond wealth's measure, a treasure of the mind.

Enchanted by flavours, deep and true,
A love unwavering, steadfast and new.
In your embrace, I'm finally home,
A love story written, no longer alone.

BETRAYAL'S BITE

Betrayal's venom, a corrosive art,
Consuming from within, tearing me apart.
A gut-wrenching rage, a primal desire,
To lash out, to burn with consuming fire.

Powerless fury, a silent scream,
A heart turned to stone, a desolate dream.
Night's embrace, a bitter, lonely keep,
As rancour's seeds in darkness creep.

RAMBLING PLEA

Often, we traverse life's path blind to the seeds we sow,
Ignorant of the growth nurtured, the burdens we bestow.
We ignite joy, quell sorrows, then abruptly depart,
Leaving echoes of shared moments, a bittersweet art.

Memories become treasures of a life well spent,
Love given freely, a tender, sweet intent.
Yet, what price for this fragile, euphoric state?
How does one prepare for loss, cruel and irate?

To surrender self, hopes, dreams on love's altar,
A gamble with destiny, a celestial caller.
Would I risk it all again or shield a part?
A poignant question.

Serendipity's hand, a cosmic decree,
Bound our lives in a tapestry, wild and free.
In moments of bliss, with you by my side,
The world faded as love's warmth I defied.

So, what's this confession, this rambling plea?
A heart laid bare, yearning for clarity.

SHIFTING TIDES

We roamed as equals, wild and free,
A brotherhood forged, strong and deep.
Now, a new chapter for you, I see,
As life's journey takes a different step.

A suit adorns you, a solemn sight,
As you embark on love's new light.
A bittersweet moment, a complex blend,
As lifelong friendships start to bend.

Though paths diverge, our bond remains,
A steadfast anchor through life's pains.
We'll cherish memories, a treasured hoard,
As you embark on life's new board.

Congratulations on this joyous day,
May love and laughter light your way.
Our friendship's a cornerstone, strong and true,
As you and yours begin anew.

CHAPTER 6

NATURE & INTROSPECTION

STEADY PULSE OF LIFE

The wind moves through the trees like a whispered memory. Sunlight fractures against the leaves, scattering gold across the forest floor. The earth beneath your feet is cool, uneven, alive with the pulse of unseen roots and crawling insects. Here, in this world that bends but does not break, we meet ourselves—raw, unguarded, and entirely present.

Listen: a stream gurgles over stones, relentless yet patient. A bird cuts across the sky, its call sharp and precise, a single note in a symphony of quiet. In the hush between breaths, shadows lengthen and shorten, revealing the contours of your own thoughts, your own fractures, your own courage. Pain and beauty exist side by side, inseparable as stone and river. The thorn pierces, the blossom opens, and your spirit learns to rise between the two.

Step lightly, not to disturb, but to feel. Touch bark with your fingertips; notice its rough patience. Press your palms to cold earth; let it anchor the tremors in your chest. Let the scents of rain, moss, and sun-warmed soil carry you into a conversation with your own heart. The forest, the field, the endless horizon—they do not judge. They simply witness. And in witnessing, you may witness yourself.

Every shadow has its lesson. Every gust of wind its counsel. Every flicker of sunlight, every tremor of leaf, every quiet rush of water, is a hand reaching out, reminding you that you are here, you are whole, you are capable of renewal.

May the earth beneath your feet remind you of your own roots, steadfast and enduring.
May the wind teach you to bend without breaking, to move gracefully through life's tempests.
May the rhythm of water, the flight of birds, the patience of stone, all guide you to stillness and clarity. May your eyes open to the small wonders you have long overlooked, and may your heart open to the strength you have always carried.

And when you rise from this reflection, may your spirit, grounded and free, feel the steady pulse of life, knowing you are seen, you are held, and you are ready. And as you leave this chapter, carrying its quiet lessons into the rest of your journey, may every step, every pause, every breath steady you as we **STAND ON OUR LAST BONES.**

FORGED IN NATURE

In solitude's embrace, I find my voice,
Unveiling depths where shadows once rejoice.
A solitary scribe, in realms unknown,
Seeking resonance, a kindred tone.

Why bare my soul to an indifferent eye?
Yet, in vulnerability, truths may lie.
Not for acclaim, but catharsis's art,
To mend the spirit, to heal the heart.

Nature's sculptor with chisel and storm,
Forges resilience, a steadfast form.
In trials, we're tempered, refined by fire,
Emerging stronger with newfound desire.

A cosmic dance, a grand design,
Where human spirit and nature intertwine.
With every challenge, a lesson to learn,
A soul ignited, a spirit to burn.

Through tempest and calm, she guides our way,
 A steadfast compass, come what may.
In her embrace, we find our place,
A symphony of life, a cosmic grace.

ZORA'S EDEN

Nature's canvas, painted with delight,
Where cool streams whisper, birds take flight.
Sun-kissed shadows dancing on the breeze,
As twilight's curtain, softly, gently, please.

Stars ignite a celestial show,
As worries fade and spirits grow.
With pen in hand, a heart set free,
Zora's spirit finds its harmony.

Happiness blooms, a fragrant, sweet bouquet,
Laughter's melody, a joyful symphony
Blissful moments cherished, pure and deep,
In dreams of solace where memories sleep.

A wish upon a star, a hopeful gleam,
Contentment found, a life's sweet dream.
Zora's smile, a radiant, sunny art,
A masterpiece born from a grateful heart.

NIGHT'S PRISONER

Two a.m.'s abyss, a drowning sea,
A nightly ritual, haunting me.
Anchored to despair, a captive soul,
Lost in shadows, where darkness takes its toll.

A whispered plea, a silent cry,
As restless thoughts fill up the sky.
Neighbours hushed, or so I hope and pray,
As tears descend with fading day.

Doctors' diagnoses, a colourful array,
Medications mask but don't allay.
Pastors' prayers, a comforting guise,
Yet sleep remains an elusive prize.

Insomnia's grip, a relentless hold,
A weary warrior, growing old and cold.
A battle waged, night after night,
Seeking solace in morning's light.

ENGLAND'S SOUL

England's soul, morning's gentle kiss,
A radiant glow, a moment's pure bliss.
Your essence seeps, a whispered, tender art,
Igniting passions, soul and mind apart.

London's grandeur, a crown upon your head,
A queenly spirit where legends are bred.
Your voice, a symphony, a haunting strain,
Inspiring hearts and easing every pain.

Like royalty, you reign with grace and might,
A beacon shining, a guiding light.
Your history echoes, a timeless lore,
A nation's heartbeat, forevermore.

A SOLITARY BLOOM

A solitary path, a journey fraught,
With hospital halls, a haunting thought.
A silent battle waged within the soul,
As shadows lengthen and spirits despair.

While others flourish, I wither and yearn,
A barren landscape, where hopes discern.
A flicker of hope, a distant star,
Amidst the darkness, I'll push so far.

Endometriosis, a relentless foe,
A heavy burden, I've come to know.
But in this struggle, I'll find my might,
To rise above with all my might.

Every challenge, I'll bravely face,
And find resilience in life's embrace.
A warrior's spirit, I'll cultivate,
To conquer shadows and celebrate.

With a steadfast heart, I'll brave the storm,
Till hope and healing find their form.
No fear shall hold, no doubt shall stay,
I'll rise renewed with each new day.

A BEACON IN THE STORM

In shadows deep, where sorrows reside,
A flicker of hope, a guiding tide.
Through pain's embrace, I find my way,
To dawn's horizon, a brighter day.

With every challenge, a spirit's test,
I'll rise above and stand the best.
Resilience forged in trials of fire,
A soul ignited with pure desire.

To conquer darkness with steadfast heart,
To play my role from the very start.
A warrior's journey, a noble quest,
With hope as a compass, I'll do my best.

So, let it be, a future bright,
To banish shadows and claim the light.
With courage as shield, I'll face the storm,
Emerging stronger, forever reborn.

FRACTURED REFLECTIONS

A kaleidoscope of shattered dreams,
Her pieces askew, like scattered beams.
Hope's fragile light swallowed whole,
I gaze inward at a fractured soul.

Heartbreak's dance, a bitter waltz,
Uniting and dividing life's cruel qualms.
A haunting echo of love's demise,
As her past's shadow, before me lies.

His laughter, a weapon, a twisted art,
Breaking her spirit, tearing her apart.
Love's twisted game, a cruel reprise,
As she searches for solace beyond his lies.

CHAPTER 7

BREATH UNBOUND, KNEES AND ECHOES OF LOUD SILENCE RISING

> We have held our breath too long. Eight minutes. Forty-six seconds. A name whispered into eternity: George Floyd. A body pressed into pavement, a life stolen, a world forced to pause. In that pause, we found both grief and fire.
>
> This chapter is the space where the personal meets the collective, where sorrow transforms into witness, where rage is sculpted into resilience. Here live the mothers who cradle fear and hope together, the sons taught vigilance as a daily practice, the daughters carrying crowns in a world that doubts their brilliance. Here live the echoes of history—slavery, segregation, microaggressions, the constant calculus of survival—but also the flames of refusal, the determination to rise, to speak, to claim space.
>
> These poems are not quiet. They are not polite. They are lungs and heart and body, bearing witness to centuries of silenced voices and stolen breaths. Step into them not as a bystander, but as someone willing to carry memory, to carry responsibility, to carry change. Step into them

ready to hear the fury, the grief, and the hope that refuses to be quiet.

May the weight of every name lift you rather than break you.
May their courage seed yours, and their grief find fertile ground in your action.
May your voice never falter, your hands never tire, your spirit never bend to oppression.
May injustice meet resistance, silence meet song, and despair meet relentless hope.
May you rise, and rise again, and hold space for every breath that has been denied.

And as you turn these pages, may every cry, every march, every act of witness steady you as we **STAND ON OUR LAST BONES.**

Ngonidzashe Diana Johns

BREATHLESS AND BOUND

Eight minutes forty-six, a haunting refrain,
George Floyd's last gasp echoing in pain.
Black lives: a mantra shouted loud and clear,
Yet shadows of injustice linger near.

Too many fallen victims of hate's cold hand,
A world divided, a fractured land.
I can't breathe: a cry that shook the core,
Igniting a fire forevermore.

A longing for innocence, a simpler time,
Before race and prejudice were haunting crimes.
A world where colour held no weight or sway,
Where dreams could flourish, come what may.

But memory's grasp tightens, a bitter pill,
A nation's wounds, festering still.
Injustice's shadow, long and deep,
Where stereotypes and prejudice creep.

A constant battle, a weary fight,
To be seen, respected, claimed as a right.
To break the chains, to rise above,
To find solace, peace, and love.

When will the day dawn when hearts unite,
Beyond the colour of skin, a blinding light?
When equality reigns and justice prevails,
And the weight of oppression finally fails.

Until that day, we'll carry on,
With hope as our shield and strength as our dawn.
For in every struggle, a chance to mend,
A world transformed, where love transcends.

Ngonidzashe Diana Johns

BREATH HELD, FISTS RAISED

Eight minutes. Forty-six seconds.
A knee on a neck.
A world holding its breath.

I can't breathe.
We can't breathe.

Say his name until the sky splits open:
George Floyd.
Say their names—
the roll call of stolen futures.
This is not a headline.
This is a body.
This is a son, a father, a friend.
Black Lives Matter.
Not a slogan. A heartbeat. A vow.

We have buried too many names in hashtags.
Too many sons taught to make themselves small
when sirens scream.
Too many mothers praying their children come home.
Too many brothers hiding their rage
behind smiles that crack their faces.
Survival as etiquette.

Standing on our Last Bones

We remember the long shadow:
the confident Black man punished for rising,
the bright Black girl mistaken for someone else,
the nappy hair touched like a curiosity,
the name on the CV changed for safety.
We carry it all in our lungs.

And yet we roar.
We roar for every Black son
who learned the weight of suspicion
before he learned to drive.
We roar for every Black mother
whose prayers are armor
and whose lullabies are warnings.

We roar for every Black man
whose body is read as weapon
no matter how he stands.
We roar for every Black woman
called "angry" for daring to speak.

We dream of a world
where we do not teach our children
how to survive a traffic stop,
where funerals are not classrooms
for hymns of Black pain,
where breath is not a gamble.

We dream of a day
when no one rehearses their humanity
to stay alive.

Eight minutes. Forty-six seconds.
A man's last breath
became a summons.
We cannot unsee.
We will not be silent.

Say their names again.
Say them until the walls crack.
Say them until laws change.
Say them until breath is free.

We were never meant to live
holding our breath.
We were meant to breathe,
to sing, to rise.

So rise.
Rise with your fists, your voices, your unbowed hearts.
Rise for the sons we could not save,
for the mothers who kept vigil,
for the bones that hold our history,
for the breath we refused to surrender.

Rise until the air trembles,
until justice is more than a whisper,
until our children inherit streets that do not fear them.
Rise until our songs shatter silence,
until our rage becomes wind, lifting us higher.

We rise.
We rise still,
on our last bones,
and we will never stop.

MAMA ANSWERS BACK

Baby,
I heard you.
Across eight minutes and forty-six seconds
I heard you call my name.
"Mama," you cried,
"I can't breathe."
My arms weren't there,
but my spirit was.
Every Black mama's spirit was.
We felt the pavement under your cheek,
we felt the knee on your neck,
we felt your breath leaving
like a bird forced from its cage.

We have carried this fear since the cradle —
raising Black sons in a world
that crosses the street at their laughter,
that mistakes their brilliance for threat.
We ironed your shirts,
we taught you your "yes sirs" and "no ma'ams,"
we prayed over you every night

so you would come home.
Still, they treated you less than a dog.

I am exhausted.
We are exhausted.
But hear me, child:
We are also a storm.
We are the drumbeat in the march,
the hands locking together in the street,
the women who bury their tears and rise anyway.
We will not let your breath be wasted.
We will tell every mama after me:
teach your boy his worth before the world tries to steal it,
teach your girl her crown before they call her "angry."
Teach them to stand, to breathe, to fight, to live.

Baby, they may have taken you,
but they did not take your name.
Your cry became a summons.
Your breath became a movement.
And the mothers of the world heard it.
We are building a world
where no child's body lies in the street,
where no mama's lullaby is a warning.
We are not done.
We are rising.

Standing on our Last Bones

So rest now, son.
Mama's here.
We're still breathing.
We're still marching.
We're still fighting
for a day when no mother
will have to answer this cry again.

RESILIENCE RISING

You wield your power like a careless toy,
Indulging ego, a cruel employ.
The voiceless suffer, their rights denied,
As shadows lengthen, where hope once died.

Zimbabwe weeps for daughters' pain,
For women's anguish, a ceaseless strain.

In silent torment, years slip away,
But from ashes, a phoenix will rise

Together, we rise, a defiant stand,
To heal the wounds across the land.

With hearts united, we'll break the chain,
And hope will triumph once more to reign.

SHATTERED REFLECTIONS

A crumbling façade, a fortress of pain,
'Strong,' they insist, a cruel refrain.
A crimson canvas where shadows reside,
Lost in the echoes where hope has died.

Years etched in suffering, a body's despair,
Time stands still, a frozen stare.
A hollowed vessel, emotions concealed,
Like shattered glass, where feelings are revealed.

Black joy eclipsed, a mournful night.
In the darkness, a flicker of light.
A battle within for a soul to mend,
On hope's frail thread, this journey transcends.

A tempest within, a silent cry,
To reach for the heavens, soaring high.
Through trials and storms his grace endures.
A steadfast anchor where hope ensures.

Ngonidzashe Diana Johns

SHACKLED SPIRIT, SOARING SOUL

Decaying walls, a canvas of despair,
Leaky taps and echoes of despair.
Thin walls, neighbours' lives laid bare,
A humble prison, yet a spirit's lair.

Flip-flop showers, a makeshift rite,
Acclimatized to shadows of the night.
Self-reflection, a silent, inward sea,
Counting months in poverty's decree.

But in this wreckage, a phoenix I find,
A spirit soaring, leaving self behind.
'Chiedza' birthed from hardship's core,
An author's voice forevermore.

With head held high, I step into the light,
From shackled hands, a future takes flight.
The irony of fate, a twisted art,
A resilient soul, a brand-new start.

IGNITE

A furnace burns within, a soulful core,
Inherited rage, forevermore.
Black woman, angry, hear my cry,
Injustice's echo, reaching for the sky.

Shackled spirits, tears that deeply sear,
Ancestral pain I carry year by year.
Battle-worn voices, whispers in my breath,
A warrior's heart, defying death.

Centuries of struggle forged my might,
A queen arose, claiming back the light.
Unsilenced, untamed, a force unleashed,
Anger's tempest, passions unreleased.

Dismiss me not, for in my ire,
A world ignites, consumed by fire.
Voice of the silenced, oppressed and torn,
A defiant anthem bravely born.

Black woman, angry, strong and deep,
From sorrow's ashes, hope I reap.
Listen closely to this rising roar,
A dawn of justice, forevermore.

ZORA'S STORM

Zora enters, a tempestuous sea
Amidst whispers, judgment's scrutiny.
A prisoner of shadows, a soul confined,
Battling demons, complex and unkind.

Karma's wheel, a cruel, relentless spin,
Traumas etched deep, scars from within.
Guilt and shame, a heavy, haunting load,
A fragile spirit, bruised and eroded.

Lullaby for Zora, hush now, darling, let sorrow cease,
Insomnia's grip, a haunting disease.
Low self-esteem, a bearish friend,
But courage flickers, a hope to mend.

CHAPTER 8

EMBERS OF BECOMING, ASHES & ALTERS

> We rise. From every fracture, every whisper of doubt, every night that seemed too long. We rise from the ashes of dreams deferred, from bones cracked and hearts tested. Twenty-five, thirty, fifty—age is just the stage. The story is ours.
>
> We rise in mirrors, reflecting not only who we were, but who we are daring to become luminous, fierce, unbowed. We rise through rites of passage, through ululations and quiet prayers, through the sacred whispers of ancestors stitched into our marrow. We rise in laughter, in tears, in the triumph of motion over limitation, in every "wheel it to will it" moment that defies expectation.
>
> We rise because we choose to. Because each struggle becomes a spark, each burden a wing, each scar a crown, each failure a lesson etched in fire. We rise in the stillness of prayer, in the breathless pursuit of dreams, in letters typed, pens lifted, voices spoken, stories shared.

We rise for ourselves and the generations behind us. For the mothers, the grandmothers, the girls learning their worth. For every body told it is too much, too fragile, too bold. For every spirit that refuses to stay silent.

So rise. Rise with the wind, rise with the tide, rise with bones that ache yet carry you higher.
Rise in joy, in rage, in mercy, in courage. Rise as a storm, as a light, as a movement, as a promise. Rise because the world will bend only to those who stand, who insist, who breathe.

And when the night falls, when doubt whispers, when the weight presses— remember, you are made of fire, forged in love, anchored in faith. You are unbroken. You are luminous. You are rising. We are not merely surviving. We are **STANDING ON OUR LAST BONES**.

Ngonidzashe Diana Johns

A FOURTEEN-YEAR-OLD'S AWAKENING

Dawn's gentle kiss, a dream's soft retreat,
Then, harsh reality's brutal street.
A shattered form, a lifeless, cold display,
Shattering innocence in the cruellest way.

Robbery, murder, war's relentless tide,
Humanity's wounds, where does hope hide?
Hunger's grip, a world in disarray,
Can peace prevail, or darkness hold sway?

Yet, in despair, a flicker of light,
Love and compassion, burning ever bright.
Equality's banner, a noble quest,
Justice for all, humanity's behest.

Who bears this burden, this heavy load?
A call to action, a sacred code.
Young hearts aflame with purpose clear,
To shape a world where peace is held dear.

With every step, a promise I make,
To build a future for humanity's sake.
Respect and kindness, seeds I'll sow,
A legacy of hope where love will grow.

TWENTY-FIVE

A mirrored reflection, child and woman entwined,
Tears blur the image, leaving heart behind.

Student loans loom, responsibilities creep,
While youthful dreams in shadowed corners sleep.

Twenty-five, a paradox of age and soul,
A masquerade of strength, a fragile whole.

The Cheshire Cat beckons, a whimsical flight,
To escape this labyrinth, to find the light.

Decisions echo, a haunting refrain,
As life unfolds, a complex terrain.

A shattered mirror, a moment of truth,
Revealing battles, youth, and future's booth.

With newfound clarity, a path unfolds,
Ambition ignites where courage boldly holds.

No longer lost in Wonderland's maze,
Twenty-five blossoms in unexpected ways.

ROORA RITUAL

A rite of passage whispered through the years,
A journey for daughters, conquering fears.
Grandmothers, mothers, paved this sacred way,
Yet each woman's story a unique display.

Ululations rise, a chorus of acclaim,
As womanhood is honoured, a hallowed name.
Family gathered, hearts filled with glee,
A daughter blossoms, wild and free.

'Makhoti, Muroora,' echoes through the land,
A cherished title bestowed by woman's hand.
Love's ember kindled, a matrimonial art,
As hearts unite, soul to soul, apart no more.

A new family found, a welcoming embrace,
A sisterhood of love in this sacred space.
Black love's magic, a potent, binding spell,
As joyous voices and laughter swell.

Beyond the custom, a personal bloom,
A woman's spirit, breaking from the womb.
In every daughter, a legacy resides,
As tradition evolves, where hope abides.

WHEEL IT TO WILL IT

Four wheels whirling,
Shadowed laughter seeping,
A spirit soaring in overdrive,
Wheel it to will it!

One, two steps on stairway rockets!
Zimmer frame in perfect stride,
Onlookers gasping, hearts igniting,
You can wheel it to will it.

Muffled cries into the void,
Reflected triumphs reverberate,
Shadowed humour sparks the muse,
While I wheel it to will it!

DIVINE REFUGE

Enveloped in shadows, guilt's cold embrace,
I seek solace, a divine space.
Omnipotent, present, knowing all,
Your outstretched hand, a saving call.

'Pray without ceasing,' echoes the plea,
Faith's compass guiding, setting me free.
With heart renewed, I rise and stand,
In Your embrace, a promised land.

A warrior's spirit, strong and bold,
Against life's tempests, a story untold.
Low self-esteem, a fleeting fear,
Your love conquers, drawing me near.

Temptation's whispers, a silent foe,
But Your grace abounds, a steadfast glow.
A little saint, a soldier of light,
Standing firm with all Your might.

OUR JOURNEY'S PAGE

Let words ignite our souls' deep quest,
As boundless realms unfold, expressed.
From campus halls to world's wide stage,
We'll write our chapters, age by age.

Through trials, we'll rise, our spirits soar,
With ink of courage, stories pour.
Guided by wisdom, nature's art,
We'll craft our legacies, heart and part.

Beyond the spotlight's fleeting gleam,
Our impact's echo, a lasting dream.
With passion's fire, let words take flight,
Igniting futures, burning bright.

With words as compass, let us chart our course,
Through life's vast ocean, we'll unleash our force.
From campus halls to world's expansive stage,
Our stories echo through time's endless page.

Through trials tempered and spirits refined,
Our words ignite a beacon for mankind.
With mentors' wisdom, nature's guiding hand,
We'll shape our destinies across the land.

Not fame we seek but impact's lasting art,
To touch the world, play a noble part.
With passion's fire and grace as our guide,
We'll write our chapters with purpose and pride.

EVOLUTION OF EXPRESSION

From parchment to pixels, a digital age,
Our modes of expression a constant stage.

With degrees in hand, we step into the fray,
Guided by mentors, come what may.

Across continents, our voices resound,
In written words, our passions abound.

With every keystroke, a story takes flight,
Illuminating minds with guiding light.

Adapting to change with steadfast grace,
We navigate challenges, a relentless pace.

From handwritten letters to online posts,
Our communication never truly lost.

In this evolution, we find our place,
Connecting hearts across time and space.

With every word, a bridge we mend,
A global community without end.

Ngonidzashe Diana Johns

THE WRITER'S ODYSSEY

With diplomas clutched and dreams unfurled,
I step into a vast, unknown world.
Echoes of wisdom, mentors' sage advice,
Ignite the spark, fueling my life's device.

From quill and ink to digital art,
Words take shape, a brand-new start.
A treasure trove of thoughts, yet undefined,
A journey embarked with open mind.

Across horizons, where cultures blend,
My written words, a steadfast friend.
In prose and verse, my spirit soars,
As storytelling's magic restores.

Challenges loom like shadows deep,
But with courage as a compass, I'll bravely keep.
A tapestry woven of joy and strife,
A hero's journey, a meaningful life.

With pen in hand, I'll shape my fate,
A writer's odyssey, sealed by fate.
In every chapter, a world to explore,
As stories unfold, forevermore.

STANDING ON OUR LAST BONES

These bones are old.
Cracked but not surrendered.
Breaking at best,
burning at worst.
Some days I swear
I see red behind my eyelids —
all the years of sheltering,
carrying to maturity,
waiting for relief that never arrives.

I long for a nest.
A quiet.
A place to unstrap hidden scars,
to hush the screeching demons,
to let the spiked feelings soften.
Caged one moment,
in flight the next.
Alone but never lonely.
Lonely but never alone.

I switch gears —
smiles hiding tears,
top-tears flowing into blankets
the color of sky at dusk.

Buckets, drops,
heavy and wonder-full.
Labour and turmoil.
Love and its bittersweet weight.

Nine months full,
half-moon hope.
Home.
Red.
Pain.
Joy.
Bliss.

At best, a nest.
At worst, poison.
I am floating between
crown-adjustment and breaking bones,
between collapse and coronation —
still standing,
still becoming,
still rising on our last bones.

ABOUT THE AUTHOR

Ngonidzashe Diana Johns is a Zimbabwean-born, British poet, writer, and chronic illness advocate whose work threads together grief, resilience, and the sacred art of becoming. Qualified in Accounting & Finance, she brings both analytical depth and lyrical insight to her creative practice, weaving poetry, memoir, and cultural remembrance into offerings that illuminate the often-invisible battles women face.

Her debut collection, *Chiedza: Reflections on Darkness, Light, and The Moments in Between,* established her as a compelling voice for tenderness and triumph. She is also the founder of Chiedza Innovations, with Chiedza Co., a creative brand dedicated to journals, healing tools, and faith-rooted spaces for women navigating chronic illness, grief, and transformation.

With *Standing on Our Last Bones,* Johns deepens her body of work—writing unflinchingly from the intersections of Black womanhood, ancestral memory, and spiritual longing. Her words affirm that even in silence and sorrow, we are still rising.

Conscious Dreams
PUBLISHING

Transforming diverse writers
into successful published authors

🌐 www.consciousdreamspublishing.com

✉ authors@consciousdreamspublishing.com

Let's connect

www.ingramcontent.com/pod-product-compliance
Lightning Source LLC
Chambersburg PA
CBHW030331080526
44584CB00012B/813